INITIALISING...

First published and distributed by
viction:workshop ltd.

viction:ary™

viction:workshop ltd.
Unit C, 7/F, Seabright Plaza,
9–23 Shell Street,
North Point, Hong Kong SAR
Website: victionary.com
Email: we@victionary.com

🄾 @victionworkshop
🄵 @victionworkshop
Bē @victionary
🄿 @victionary

Edited and produced by viction:workshop ltd.

Creative Direction: Victor Cheung
Design: Scarlet Ng
Editorial: Ynes Filleul, YL Lim
Coordination: Emily Wong, Jeanie Choy,
Katherine Wong, Mavis Chan, Yan Wai Yin
Production: Bryan Leung

Cover illustration by Tom Burkewitz

ISBN 978-988-75666-5-6
Printed and bound in China

Acknowledgements
We would like to specially thank all the artists and
illustrators who are featured in this book for their
significant contribution towards its compilation. We
would also like to express our deepest gratitude
to our producers for their invaluable advice and
assistance throughout this project, as well as the
many professionals in the creative industry who were
generous with their insights, feedback, and time. To
those whose input was not specifically credited or
mentioned here, we also truly appreciate your support.

Future Editions
If you wish to participate in viction:ary's future projects
and publications, please send your portfolio to:
we@victionary.com

FUTURIA
ART OF THE SCI-FI AGE

210 × 285
MM

254
PP

SBN
9789887566656

PUBLISHED & EDITED
BY VICTIONARY

PREFACE

Since the birth of the Science Fiction genre, our collective imagination has been inexorably drawn toward the allure of the future, beckoning us to explore the uncharted realms of what might be. In these intricate narratives, their creators have crafted worlds that resonate with our own reality yet remain intriguingly different, and urge us to question, wonder, and imagine.

Futuria is an invitation to partake in a voyage through the boundless expanse of the future, as seen through the eyes of artists and illustrators who have mastered the art of world-building. Inspired by the narratives in Sci-Fi video games, comic books, television shows, and movies, each art piece is a window to landscapes both familiar and alien, inviting us to step through and explore realms not yet charted by the compass of reality.

In the pages of this book, you will embark on a journey of three portals — each its own kaleidoscope of futuristic visions relating to its respective sub-genre. Before you begin exploring the Cyberpunk Portal, brace yourself for the downpour of heavy rain as you traverse down bustling streets lit by reflections of giant neon signs flickering against the crowded pavements. As you admire the awe-inducing view of hovercrafts zipping through towering skyscrapers and winding highways, feel the frenetic energy of the city pulse through your veins. Don't forget to look down and dive into the dark underbelly — where rebels, punks, and hackers thrive in graffiti-covered alleyways and smoggy slums, hidden from the keen eyes of surveillance of the technological utopia above.

The landscapes in the Post-apocalyptic Portal lay bare the aftermath of humanity's trials and tribulations. As you wander through these desolate domains, you will encounter dilapidated buildings, abandoned towns, and collapsed infrastructure. On the other side of this stark reality is the glimmer of hope — a sign of civilisation from the warm campfires and tents amidst the ruins, exploration troops rummaging in the rubble, and survivors forging new paths in the wake of destruction. Through the eyes of each artist, experience the resilience of the human spirit amid the formidable terrains, and what beauty can emerge from the ashes.

Blurring the boundaries between the organic and synthetic is the Artificial Portal: a testament to the boundless imagination of creators who envision realities that bend the laws of nature. Strap on your spacesuit, as you prepare to wander across a hyper-futuristic world with sleek hoverboards and mesmerising holograms, inhabited by mechanical beasts and cyborgs. Here, the concept of what it means to be human takes on new, thrilling dimensions, as the advances of artificial intelligence, virtual realities, transhumanism, and biotechnological wonders challenge the very notion of existence itself.

Whether you find yourself navigating the signs and lights of Cyberpunk mega-cities, treading softly through the Post-apocalyptic wastelands, or soaring through the limitless skies of Artificial metropolises, remember that you are also traversing through the labyrinths of imagination conceived in the minds of talented creatives from around the world. While you do so, you're also invited to conjure up new frontiers of your own while envisioning an alternate future of possibilities.

Welcome to the junction of three extraordinary universes in Futuria, dear traveller — your adventure awaits.

INDEX

SPECIAL FEATURE

SHOWCASE

GAL BARKAN

Based in Tel-Aviv, Gal Barkan is a multidisciplinary artist, visual designer, art director, and musician who crafts detailed, futuristic metropolises and fantasy worlds. Inspired by cosmology, Sci-Fi films, and diverse genres of music ranging from classical to heavy metal, his art features floating cities, flying cars, and neon-lit architecture that showcase a dystopian vision of future beauty. Drawing from his background in architectural 3D visualisation, Barkan's distinct style is a result of creative evolution, where different artistic directions are explored and merged. His interest in cosmology and music deeply influences his work, with his visuals often corresponding to musical themes. His dream is to dedicate more time to creating immersive experiences that merge his audio and visual worlds through film and media.

11
Biocities Nights [T]
Adobe Photoshop, Autodesk 3ds Max [S]

What prompted you to start creating works inspired by Sci-Fi, and how did you develop your current style?

I have always been captivated by the genres of science fiction and fantasy. The manner in which a book, film, or even an image can transport you into a completely different reality, wholly conceived by its creator, has always fascinated me.

From a young age, I was drawn to the creation of futuristic landscapes and imaginative worlds. I developed an interest in computers early on and commenced my journey into the world of 3D and digital art. My interest in architecture led me to delve into architectural visualisation. Here, I refined my skills to craft expansive urban landscapes. Over time, this acquired knowledge and skillset naturally found their way into my personal artwork.

Where does the inspiration for your work come from? What other artists, movies or books inspire you the most?

My inspiration comes from many places: classical artwork, books, films, contemporary artists, nature, and a wide array of music. Being a music creator, I've found that composing stimulates my imagination, and help me dream up new worlds. In turn, the visuals I make also spark new musical ideas. All of these aspects blend together into the personal universe that I've been building.

In my work, you'll find traces of inspiration from various places. There are elements from films like 'Blade Runner', 'Alien', '2001: A Space Odyssey' and many more. Concept artists such as Syd Mead and H.R. Giger, as well as Sci-Fi books by acclaimed authors like Arthur C. Clarke, Isaac Asimov, Frank Herbert, and others have also influenced me. As for music, the list is endless — from classical tunes to rock, progressive rock, to electronic beats.

Can you tell us a bit more about your creative and production process? How do you first visualise the concept of each piece?

Usually, I start with a vision in my mind of what I wish to create. At times, I might browse the web to find inspiring visuals, which I save for reference in terms of style or technique. Occasionally, I review my existing portfolio to consider how I can translate my initial vision into a tangible image. Following that, I open the 3D software or other tools I use and start experimenting. I create numerous real-time renders and sketches until I discover the visual that resonates with my original concept. Lately, I've been utilising artificial intelligence (AI) tools for various stages of my creative process, ranging from the initial conceptual phase to the final output.

What are the differences between working on personal passion projects and client work? How do you maintain a balance between the two?

Working on personal projects is the most rewarding part of my artistic journey. Over the years, my professional work has demanded a significant amount of my time and energy. In the past, I could only devote evenings and weekends to my art. However, I've recently had the privilege to shift my focus entirely to creating my personal projects and worlds. This opportunity to invest my full attention and time into my art has been truly fulfilling.

With the rapid development of imaging technology and virtual reality, have you ever imagined your work experienced in a newer, more immersive way?

I enjoy exploring new and emerging technologies, always considering anything that could help bring my ideas to life. Over the years, I've experimented with a variety of technologies, including 360 visuals accompanied by original music and real-time interactive forms of virtual reality (VR). I'm interested in integrating my work, both in visuals and music, into these immersive experiences. Recently, I've also ventured into using AI for creating visuals and videos. I hold the belief that any medium capable of manifesting your ideas into reality deserves exploration.

Your portfolio consists mainly of sceneries of sprawling neon cities and towering buildings gleaming in neon signs and lights. Were you always interested in the Sci-Fi and Cyberpunk aesthetic, or was that something you developed along your career?

I've always been drawn to this type of aesthetic. Even as a child, I enjoyed sketching images of futuristic cities, mechanical beings, and fantasy worlds. These drawings were often accompanied by an electronic or symphonic musical soundtrack playing in my mind.

15
Nightview [T]
Adobe Photoshop, Autodesk 3ds Max [S]

16
Bioluminocities [T]
Adobe Photoshop, Autodesk 3ds Max [S]

17
Bioluminocities [T]
Adobe Photoshop, Autodesk 3ds Max [S]

Gal Barkan

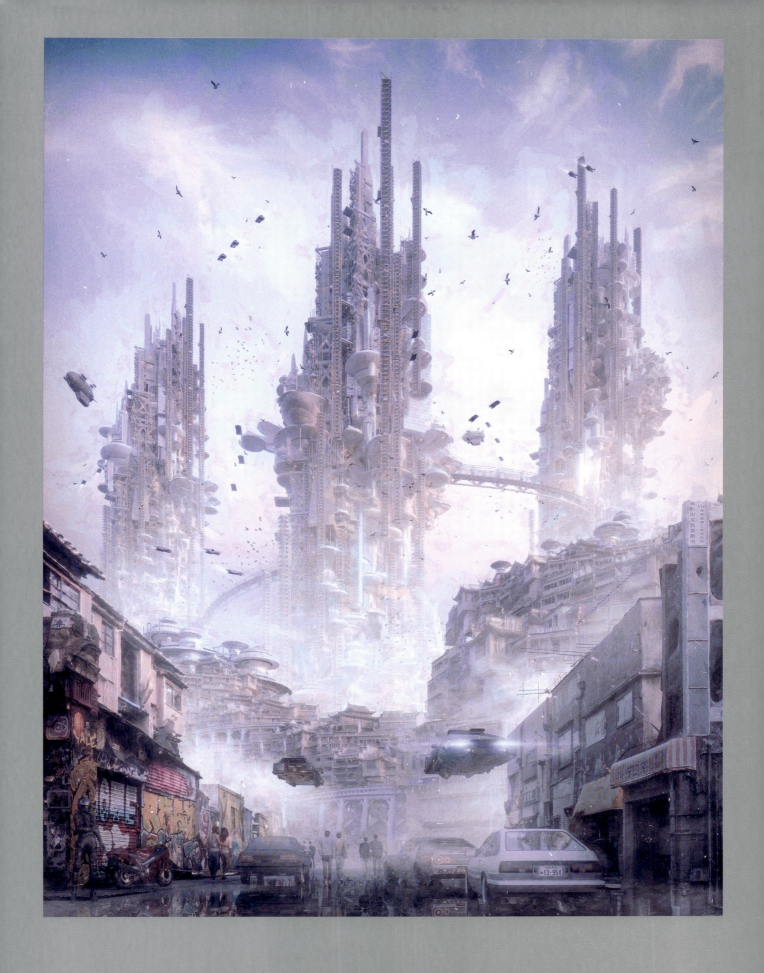

18
Art District [T]
Adobe Photoshop, Autodesk 3ds Max [S]

19
Morning Mist [T]
Adobe Photoshop, Autodesk 3ds Max [S]

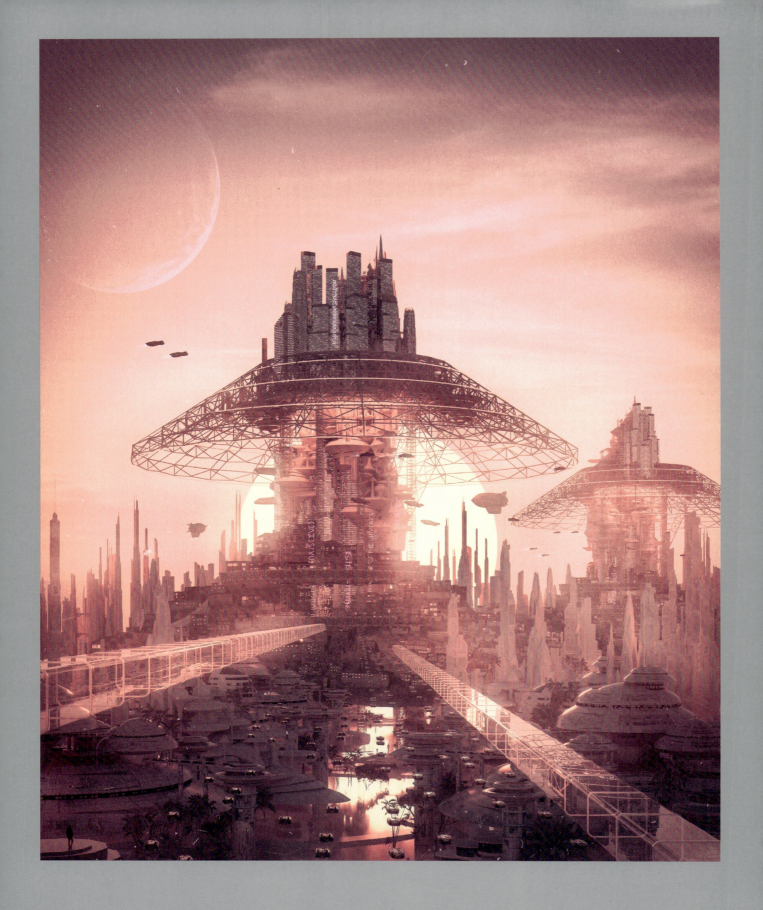

Gal Barkan

Upon closer look at your landscapes, one would usually spot a lone person or a small group of people being dwarfed by their surroundings. What emotions or feelings are you aiming to evoke through this imagery?

In my work, I aim to evoke feelings of wonder, awe, and mystery — similar to the emotions stirred when one stands before an inspiring panorama or gazes at the cosmos. While the vastness of the natural world can make an individual feel small and humbled, there's also the realisation that they hold control over their destiny and possess the capacity to create their own endless worlds within this immense universe.

What do you think the future would look/be like 1,000 years from now? What would you like/dislike about it if you could pay it a visit?

Our current reality clearly shows how challenging it is to predict what will happen a year from now, let alone a thousand years into the future. I imagine that we might see some form of symbiotic hybrid merger between humans and AI. I'd like to envision humans evolving beyond our present state of constant internal conflict and everyday struggles, possibly reaching a stage where technology has freed humanity from the routine concerns over food, shelter, and energy. Ideally, the technologies we're developing in these compelling times would meet every need, enabling us to pursue our true passions, unlock new capabilities, or simply enjoy life. If cities remain the primary human habitat, I'd like to see more integration of nature, along with a blend of technology and biology that enriches the lives of future city dwellers. The rapid advancements in AI technology could perhaps be key in creating a world that is more in harmony with nature.

To bring their own unique visual worlds of the future to life, what can artists/illustrators do to find their creative spark and build on their imagination?

Focus on areas that captivate your interest or hold personal significance. Find what excites and inspires you, absorb these ideas, and apply them using available tools, techniques, and technologies. Do it in a way that fuels your desire to keep creating and exploring your concepts.

22
Radiocity [T]
Adobe Photoshop, Autodesk 3ds Max [S]

23
Highrise [T]
Adobe Photoshop, Autodesk 3ds Max [S]

Gal Barkan

Qin Shi

26
Urban Jungle [T]
Cinema 4D, OctaneRender [S]

27
Last Sunset [T]
Cinema 4D, OctaneRender [S]

Dangiuz

28
Crossroads [T]
Cinema 4D, OctaneRender [S]

29
Suburban Nights [T]
Cinema 4D, OctaneRender [S]

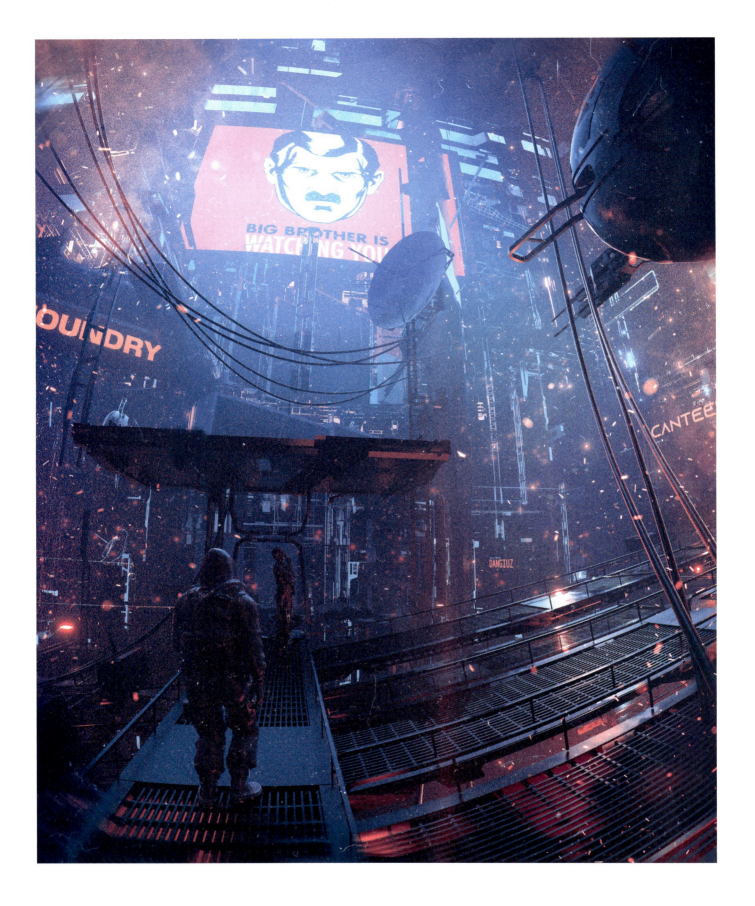

BIG BROTHER IS WATCHING YOU

32
1984 [T]
Cinema 4D, OctaneRender [S]

33
Best Friends [T]
Cinema 4D, OctaneRender [S]

Vladimir Manyukhin

34–35
Cathedral City [T]
Adobe Photoshop, Autodesk 3ds Max [S]

Vladimir Manyukhin

Jarvinart

38
Prologue [T]
Adobe Photoshop, Autodesk 3ds Max,
Chaos Corona [S]

39
Golden Gate: Arcadia [T]
Adobe Photoshop, Autodesk 3ds Max,
Chaos Corona, Procreate [S]

40
Bronze Gate: Downtown [T]
Adobe Photoshop, Autodesk 3ds Max,
Chaos Corona, Procreate [S]

41
Silver Gate: Ride Into Midnight [T]
Adobe Photoshop, Autodesk 3ds Max,
Chaos Corona, Procreate [S]

Jarvinart

42–43
Down the Rabbit Hole [T]
Adobe Photoshop, Autodesk 3ds Max, Chaos Corona, Procreate [S]

44–45
Tokyo Techno Dreams [T]
Adobe Photoshop, Autodesk 3ds Max, Chaos Corona [S]
Noe Alonzo [SC]

46–47
Edge City [T]
Adobe Photoshop, Autodesk 3ds Max, Chaos Corona, Procreate [S]

Tom Hisbergue

48-49
Neo Red Light District [T]
Adobe Photoshop [S]

Darwin Cellis

51
Guild Extractors [T]
3DCoat, Adobe Photoshop, Blender [S]

Lazaro

52
Disconnected [T]
Adobe Photoshop, Blender [S]

53
The End Of Innocence [T]
Adobe Photoshop, Blender [S]

54
Longing [T]
Adobe Photoshop, Blender [S]

55
La Galleria [T]
Adobe Photoshop, Blender [S]

Hardy Fowler

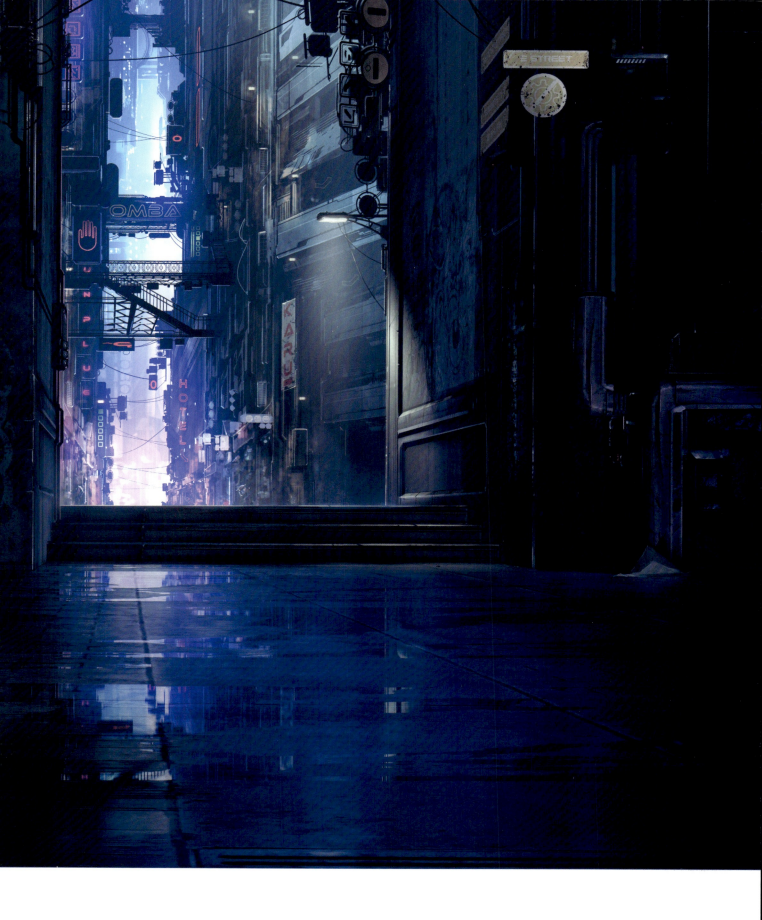

56–57
Neon District Background Art [T]
Adobe Photoshop [S]
Blockade Games [C]

Sergii Golotovskyi

Vladimir Manyukhin

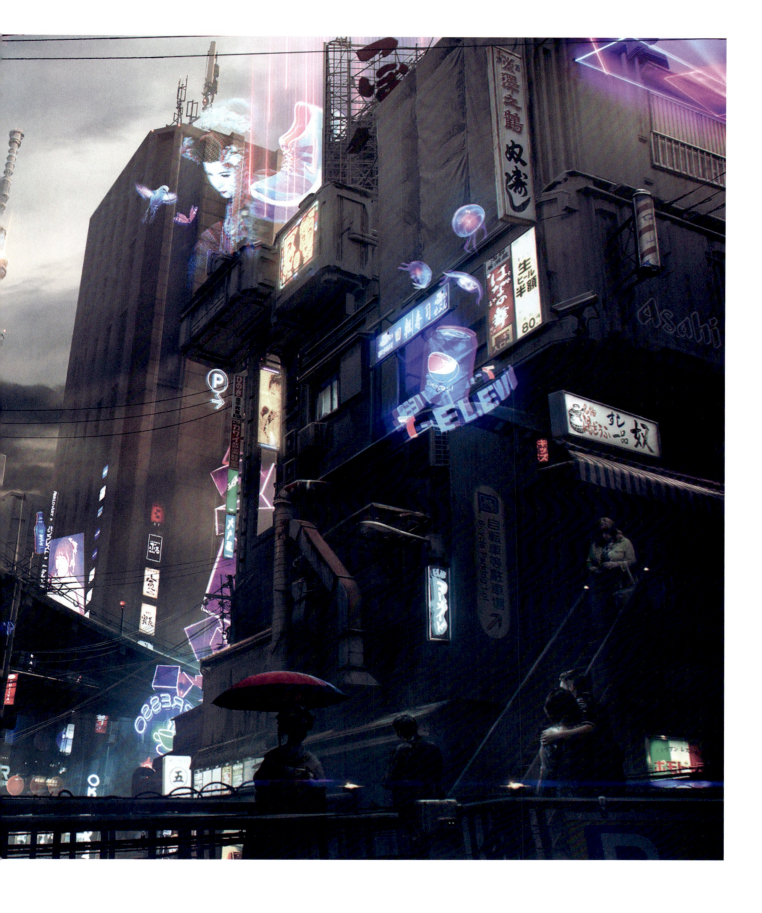

60–61
Neo Tokyo [T]
Adobe Photoshop, Autodesk 3ds Max [S]

Tom Hisbergue

SlumB [T]
Adobe Photoshop [S]

64-66
City [T]
Cinema 4D, Mol 3D, OctaneRender [S]

67
Big Den [T]
Adobe Substance 3D Painter,
Cinema 4D, Houdini, OctaneRender [S]

68
Liberty Apartments [T]
Adobe Substance 3D Painter,
Cinema 4D, Houdini, OctaneRender [S]

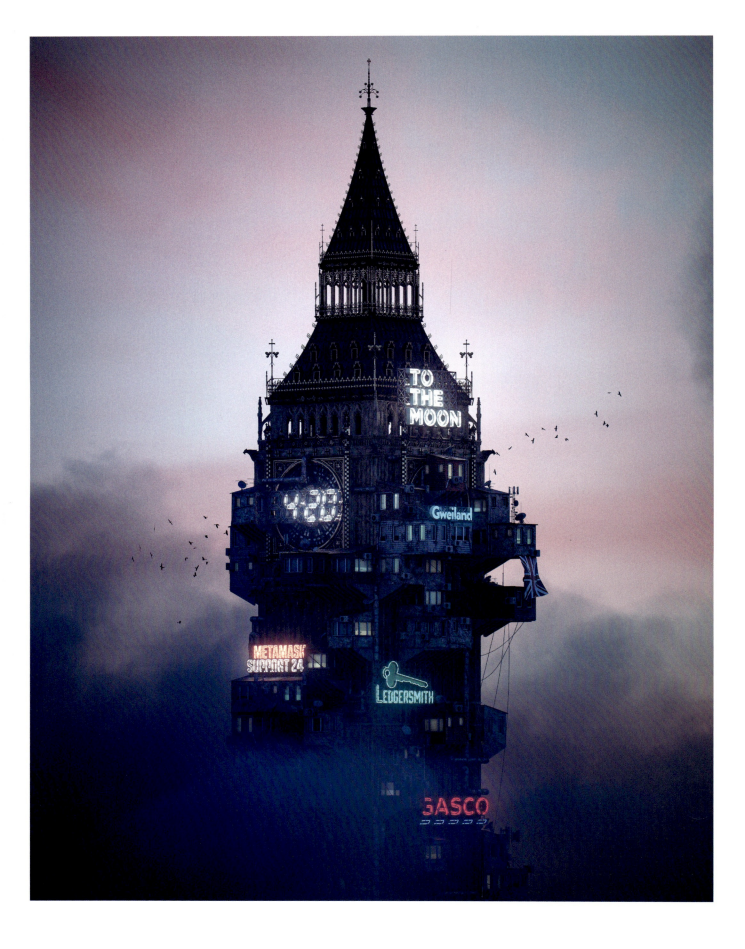

Filip Hodas

The Leaning Block [T]
Adobe Substance 3D Painter,
Cinema 4D, Houdini, OctaneRender [S]

Space Meerkat

Space Meerkat

Hélio Frazão

Hélio Frazão

76–77
Beyond Human — Main Street [T]
Adobe Photoshop, Modo [S]

Hélio Frazão

78–79
Underpass [T]
Adobe Photoshop [S]

Hardy Fowler

80–81
Neon District Background Art [T]
Adobe Photoshop [S]
Blockade Games [C]

Vladimir Manyukhin

82–83
District [T]
Adobe Photoshop, Autodesk 3ds Max [S]

Darya Laziuk

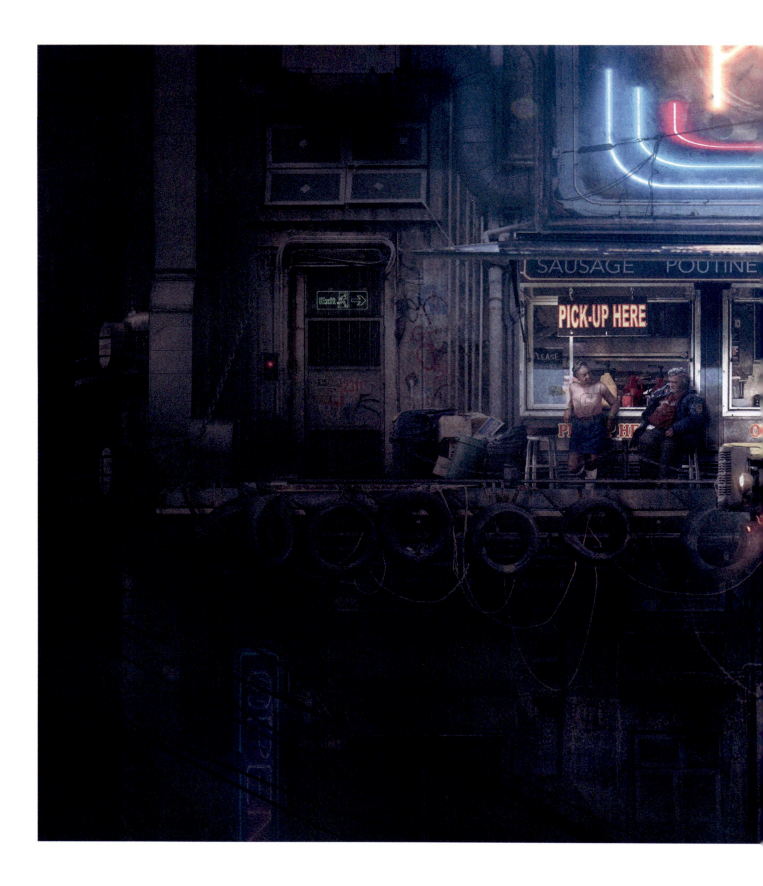

Tom Hisbergue

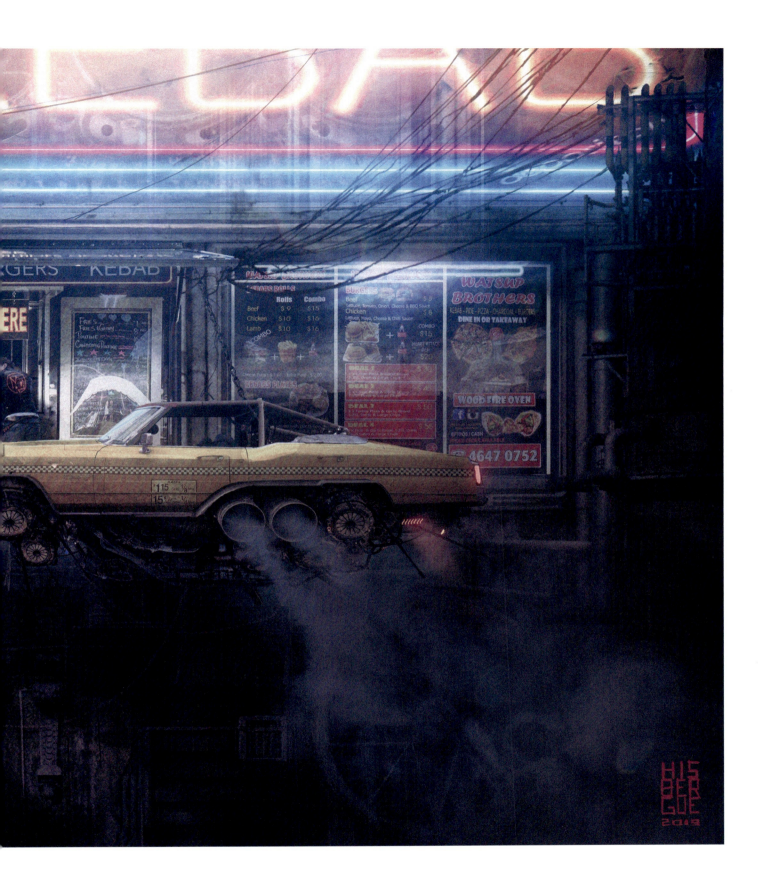

Stanislav Verbitsky

SPECIAL FEATURE

SHOWCASE

FILIP HODAS

Filip Hodas, a digital artist based in Prague, balances on the edge between reality and fiction through intricate 3D renderings. In 2015, he started a daily rendering project that lasted over 400 days, garnering an online following of over 600,000 fans globally. Renowned for his 'Popculture Dystopia' series, Hodas envisions deteriorating pop culture icons in post-apocalyptic settings. His widespread recognition has led to collaborations with major brands like Adidas, Apple, and Samsung, as well as artists such as Jean-Michel Jarre – while several of his renderings have achieved viral status, gracing the front pages of numerous websites and social platforms. Hodas' art has also been showcased in galleries worldwide, including London's Tate Modern.

93
Stu's Afterparty [T]
Adobe Illustrator, Adobe Photoshop, Adobe
Substance 3D Designer, Adobe Substance
3D Painter, Agisoft Metashape, Cinema 4D,
OctaneRender [S]

Filip Hodas

94
No-laf [T]
Adobe Illustrator, Adobe Photoshop, Adobe
Substance 3D Designer, Adobe Substance
3D Painter, Agisoft Metashape, Cinema 4D,
OctaneRender [S]

95
Rusty Metal Ass [T]
Adobe Illustrator, Adobe Photoshop, Adobe
Substance 3D Designer, Adobe Substance 3D
Painter, Cinema 4D, OctaneRender [S]

What prompted you to start creating works inspired by Sci-Fi, and how did you develop your current style?

I was always a fan of Sci-Fi and fantasy media, so it was pretty natural to reflect that in my work. My style is quite fluent and I like to keep it fresh and try new things, so it's a never-ending process.

Where does the inspiration for your work come from? What other artists, movies, or books inspire you the most?

It varies so much it is hard to pinpoint one thing! It can be anything from walking past a random building to a silly joke or a TV show. A lot of my work is inspired by cartoons and my childhood. I was always very inspired by surrealists, especially Dali and Magritte — I think that is very visible in my older pieces. I also like to take a lot of inspiration from architecture, having had a period of doing a lot of brutalism-influenced work. Of course, I'm also inspired by current digital artists like Ian McQue, Marek Denko, Cornelius Dämmrich, Beeple, Sparth, Simon Stålenhag, and many more.

It's really good to be open-minded and try to look outside of your bubble.

Can you tell us a bit more about your creative and production process? How do you first visualise the concept of each piece?

I usually jump straight into 3D and do a block out with basic shapes, and then one-by-one I work on the individual assets, slowly adding details and texturing and placing them into the scene. I adjust the whole scene as I go along, based on how the pieces fit together.

What are the differences between working on personal passion projects and client work? How do you maintain a balance between the two?

I quite enjoy working on both, as long as the client work aligns with my vision at least a little bit and the client trusts me.

Sometimes it can be quite hard to say no to a job and focus on personal work instead, but I feel it is important to explore and learn new things outside of client projects.

I usually deliver the entire project for my clients; I don't really do day rate/external studio jobs very often, so it can be challenging to strike a balance. I can land two big jobs in a

Bikini Bottom [T]
Adobe Illustrator, Adobe Photoshop, Adobe
Substance 3D Designer, Adobe Substance 3D
Painter, Cinema 4D, OctaneRender [S]

(often including weekends) and then have no projects work out for the next two months afterward, so I have to allocate my time based on that.

With the rapid development of imaging technology and virtual reality, and the metaverse, have you ever imagined your work experienced in a newer, more immersive way?

Of course, I have been exploring that a lot and definitely plan to dip my toes into some immersive stuff. I just want to make sure the experience will be truly realistic, like my work is, and not a low-res, cut down version of it, which still often is the case today.

Your works often feature desolate landscapes with dilapidated structures of well-known cartoon characters from popular culture. Why did you choose these characters to include in your work, and what part do they play in your universe?

As a kid from Eastern Europe who grew up without cable TV, a lot of these Disney characters were really special to me and I would religiously watch them every morning on Saturday and Sunday from 7–9 a.m. because that was the only time they were on Czech TV back in the 90s. I have very fond memories of these cartoons and it's nice to reminisce and dip into a bit of nostalgia.

Upon looking at some of your architecture-focused work, the towering buildings are often juxtaposed with real-life structures such as Big Ben and the Statue of Liberty. What kind of narrative were you aiming to tell through these interesting compositions?

Architecture is one of my big inspirations, so I like to include it in my work quite often. In terms of this specific series, I wanted to poke fun at the contrast between well-known picturesque landmarks and the living situation of a majority of people on Earth. I imagined a world where people would even colonise those landmarks. Everyone would be living mostly online anyway, so there was no need for big, fancy houses.

98
Kaonashi Shrine [T]
Adobe Illustrator, Adobe Photoshop, Adobe Substance 3D Designer, Adobe Substance 3D Painter, Agisoft Metashape, Cinema 4D, OctaneRender [S]

Filip Hodas

100
Vandal [T]
Adobe Illustrator, Adobe Photoshop, Adobe
Substance 3D Designer, Adobe Substance
3D Painter, Agisoft Metashape, Cinema 4D,
OctaneRender [S]

101
Mushroom Machines [T]
Adobe Illustrator, Adobe Photoshop, Adobe
Substance 3D Designer, Adobe Substance 3D
Painter, Cinema 4D, OctaneRender [S]

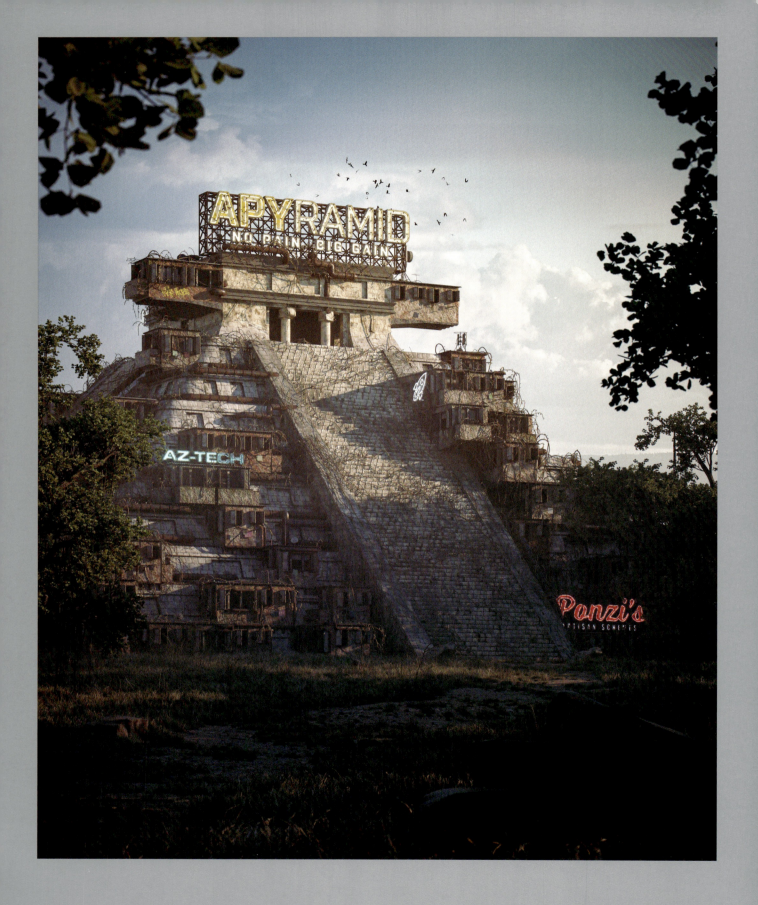

Filip Hodas

102
Apyramid [T]
Adobe Illustrator, Adobe Photoshop,
Cinema 4D, Houdini, OctaneRender [S]

103
Swinx [T]
Adobe Illustrator, Adobe Photoshop, Adobe
Substance 3D Painter, Cinema 4D, Houdini,
OctaneRender [S]

What do you think the future would look/be like 1,000 years from now? What would you like/dislike about it if you could pay it a visit?

I do believe that society will become more and more digital, to a point where the real world could genuinely mean 'less' to the average person — which I think is in many cases already happening. For example, gaming scores and the number of social media followers often mean more to the younger generation these days than accomplishments in the real world!

I'd definitely be excited about new tech developments, but I think I might dislike the societal impact of living mostly in the digital realm.

To bring their own unique visual worlds of the future to life, what can artists/illustrators do to find their creative spark and build on their imagination?

Personally, I'm a big believer in just doing things and trying stuff out. The spark and ideas usually come as a byproduct of working on things.

I learned this time and time again in pretty much everything I've ever tried. Digital art, photography, video, cooking, travelling, sport, investing...

There certainly is a lot of value in having the theoretical background and knowledge and thinking/looking for inspiration, but personal, practical experience in the field — even if it was a failure — can provide a completely different level of insight and lead to new things down the line.

105
The Treasury [T]
Adobe Illustrator, Adobe Photoshop, Adobe
Substance 3D Painter, Cinema 4D, Houdini,
OctaneRender [S]

Filip Hodas

106–107
The Stranded Robot [T]
3DCoat, Blender [S]

Xiangzhao Xi

111
The Abandoned Robot [T]
3DCoat, Adobe Photoshop, Blender [S]

Xiangzhao Xi

112–113
Mecha in the Swamp [T]
Adobe Photoshop, Blender [S]

Xiangzhao Xi

Vladimir Manyukhin

Fang Yi

Domenico Sellaro

POST-APOCALYPTIC PORTAL

Domenico Sellaro

Domenico Sellaro

Vladimir Manyukhin

Dmytro Bessonov

128-129
Fireplace [T]
3DCoat, Adobe Photoshop, Marmoset Toolbag [S]

Dmytro Bessonov

Dmytro Bessonov

Giulia Gentilini

134–135
Sunny Day [T]
Adobe Photoshop, Blender [S]

Giulia Gentilini

136–137
Mission to Minerva: Failed [T]
Adobe Photoshop, Blender [S]

Giulia Gentilini

138–139
Mission to Minerva: Failed Part 2 [T]
Adobe Photoshop, Blender [S]

Andrii Vasyliev

Vladimir Manyukhin

142–143
The Grand Canal [T]
Adobe Photoshop, Autodesk 3ds Max [S]

Petter Steen

144–145
Soviet Off World Recon Mission #1 [T]
Adobe Substance 3D Painter, Autodesk Maya, Clarisse iFX, Nuke [S]

Ede László

146–147
Sci-Fi Garage [T]
Adobe Photoshop, Blender, Cinema 4D, OctaneRender [S]

Amir Zand

148
Exodus [T]
Adobe Photoshop [S]

149
Wandering Earth [T]
Adobe Photoshop [S] KADOKAWA [C] Tamako Gunji [E] Liu Cixin [A]

Pablo Muñoz Gómez

150–151
GroundWork — Edge Colony [T]
Adobe Photoshop, KeyShot, ZBrush [S]

Thu Berchs

152–153
Inside the Ring of Phobos [T]
Adobe Photoshop, Blender, OctaneRender, World Creator [S]

Thu Berchs

Elia Pellegrini

Gate for Light — Ancient Future [T]
Adobe Photoshop, Cinema 4D, OctaneRender [S]

Elia Pellegrini

Elia Pellegrini

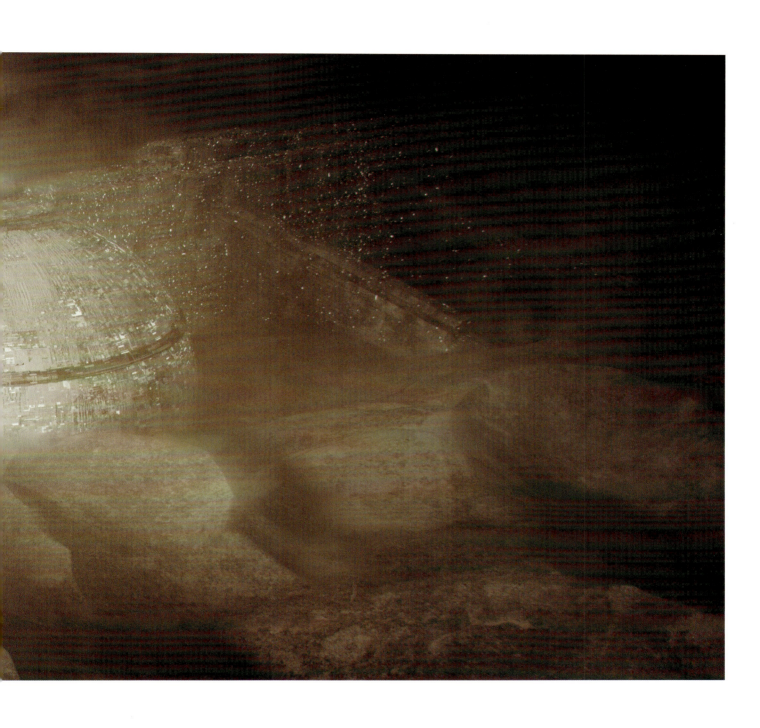

Elia Pellegrini

Elia Pellegrini

Tom Burkewitz

Tom Burkewitz

168–169
The Catcher — Harvest [T]
Adobe Photoshop (matte painting), Chaos V-Ray, SketchUp [S]

SPECIAL FEATURE

SHOWCASE

ALBERT RAMON PUIG

Albert Ramon Puig has been building his futuristic universe with its own planets, civilisations, and stories for over a decade. A 15-year veteran in the video game industry who moved from mobile to PC and console platforms, he started out as an artist and is now working as an art director — having contributed to well-known titles such as the Asphalt series, Payday 2, Overkill's The Walking Dead, and Lords of the Fallen in the course of his career. Besides playing Warhammer and tabletop games in his spare time, Puig also collects art books and listens to alternative ambient music to immerse himself in his imaginative world.

173
Vertical Favela Complex [T]
Adobe Photoshop (hand painting and photobashing) [S]

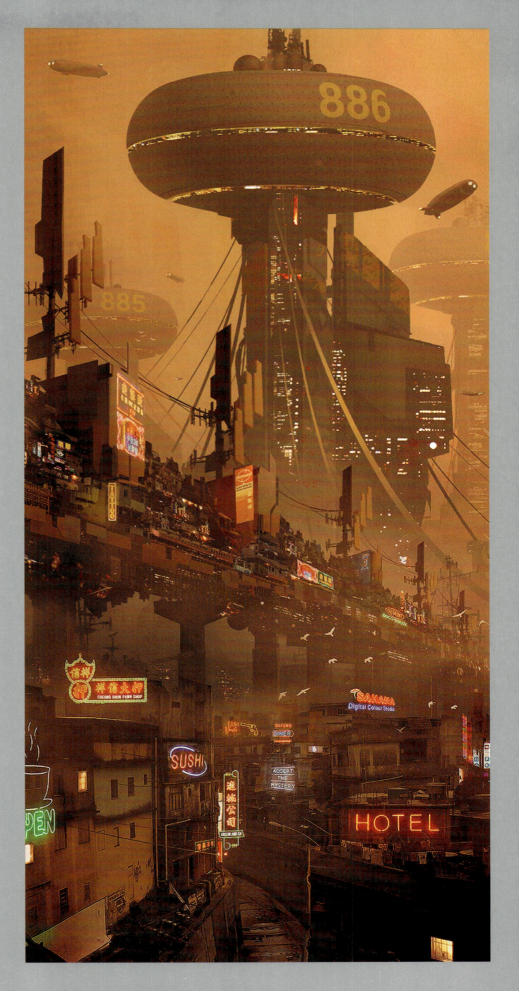

Albert Ramon Puig

174–175
Advanced Sea Lab Cellsius Corp [T]
Adobe Photoshop (hand painting and photobashing) [S]

Albert Ramon Puig

176–177
Anti-gravity Advanced Labs [T]
Adobe Photoshop (hand painting and photobashing) [S]

What prompted you to start creating works inspired by Sci-Fi, and how did you develop your current style?

I was inspired to delve into the realm of science fiction illustration by crafting landscapes rooted in our reality yet infused with futuristic technology. My aim is to explore the 'what if' scenarios, such as envisioning the consequences of colonising an icy world. In this process, I construct environments using imaginary technology that could conceivably become a reality in a distant future.

Where does the inspiration for your work come from? What other artists, movies or books inspire you the most?

My inspiration stems from movies, books, and video games, including works like 'Alien', 'Elysium', 'Dune', 'Total Recall', and 'Robocop'. I also draw inspiration from the captivating worlds of Japanese anime films from the 80s-90s, such as Akira, Gundam, Roujin Z, Patlabor, and Ghost in the Shell. Additionally, video games like Deus Ex: Human Revolution, the Fallout saga, Halo, the Metal Gear Solid saga, Mass Effect, and Wolfenstein: Colossus have also played a part in shaping my artistic vision.

Can you tell us a bit more about your creative and production process? How do you first visualise the concept of each piece?

When I create an environment, the first thing I do is create a background, imagine how people would live there if it were real, and what daily life would be like. I do a lot of sketches on paper and in notebooks for a few days before I start working in digital. I really like to create a story and a very exhaustive background of the place, so I look for references and current technologies for inspiration.

What are the differences between working on personal passion projects and client work? How do you maintain a balance between the two?

I think the difference between personal work and work for a client is that the client has a very concrete or approximate commercial vision of what he needs. He adds references, or limitations to the work so as to not deviate from the commercial objective. In the end, it is a piece of work with limitations in creativity, time, and style. I would dare to say that in a job for a client, having the technique and experience to solve the objectives of the job and knowing how to work in a team with external art direction are very important.

On the other hand, personal projects do not have commercial objectives, as they are just about capturing an idea on a canvas without restrictions or time. They are for enjoying the process of creation, and giving visual form to my imagination without limit.

With the rapid development of imaging technology and virtual reality, have you ever imagined your work experienced in a newer, more immersive way?

The truth is that with today's digital technology, I would love to be able to make my 3D environments navigable, movable and explorable someday — but that takes a lot of time to do, and there is still a lot of knowledge that I lack. I have dreamed more than once of being able to be in my environments and explore them or continue to create them from the inside.

Your futuristic landscapes and megacities often feature large spherical architecture. Are there any specific meanings behind these structures, and what part do they play in your universe?

The giant domes or spheres in my universe contain the core or generator energy and are able to cool themselves, similar to atomic power plants. In this universe, electricity is generated by gravitational engines of a material called Trythonite, which is used throughout the planetary system so it is commonly seen in the environments I design. The sizes depend on the power and model of the reactor. The larger ones run on Solid Trythonite, which is very powerful and unstable. The smaller ones down to the portable ones run on the liquid version of the material or variants of it, so they are more stable. The beam reactor models are capable of sending electricity from the planet to the space stations.

Could you introduce our readers to your rendering techniques, characteristics, and challenges? Why is it so appealing to you?

The first thing I do is develop the whole idea by sketching on paper or digital. Once I am clear about what I want, I start modelling in 3D — designing with real measurements and size references.

While I'm modelling, I create a library of textures made in Adobe Photoshop by photobashing and apply them onto the texture of the model.

After this process is done, I illuminate and separate the 3D

180–181
Alpha Complex Hangar 8 [T]
Adobe Photoshop (hand painting and photobashing) [S]

Albert Ramon Puig

elements into layers. I then generate renders and finalise them by photobashing.

I work quite methodically, with the most time-consuming phase being the initial sketching, where I meticulously iterate on the design and carefully consider every aspect of the environment. Often, not all elements are fully pre-designed, as it can get pretty overwhelming, so I prefer to reserve certain details for future concepts.

What do you think the future would look/be like 1,000 years from now? What would you like/dislike about it if you could pay it a visit?

In the future, approximately 1000 years from now, I believe that humanity will have expanded throughout our solar system, at least to the moon, and there will be humans born in space with genetic mutations, among other adaptations. I think that Earth will become more hostile in many parts due to climate change, but it will also be much more technologically advanced than it is now, thanks to the resources from space.

What I would like to see is further human evolution in every sense, including increased longevity and fewer health problems. Unfortunately, what I wouldn't like to witness is the negative side of this scenario, such as the likelihood that other civilisations will remain impoverished and a generally polarised world.

To bring their own unique visual worlds of the future to life, what can artists/illustrators do to find their creative spark and build on their imagination?

I believe that artists and aspiring artists should start imagining universes with their pros and cons in order to stimulate their brains and seek solutions in those fantasy worlds. For example, in a world where the population possesses anti-gravitational technology, they could contemplate the advantages and disadvantages of everyone living in flight while the terrestrial realm becomes more like a landfill. I think that when we imagine overly perfect universes, we lose originality. However, if we imagine more realistic universes with their consequences, it forces us to think about how to solve them and generates a lot more content and imagination.

Another important aspect is not relying too heavily on AI or excessive references. It's crucial to experiment, conduct thorough research, and create sketches. Ultimately, imagination can be trained and developed over time.

Albert Ramon Puig

182–183
Neoshaguawam City Canal Gates [T]
Adobe Photoshop (hand painting and photobashing) [S]

Albert Ramon Puig

Gal Barkan

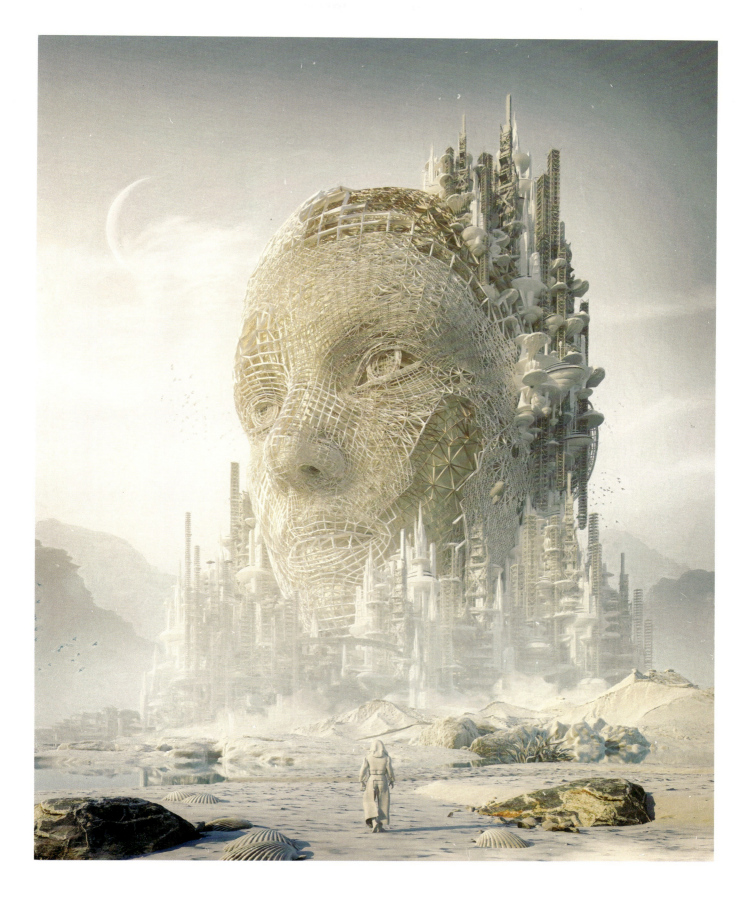

186
Future Times [T]
Adobe Photoshop, Autodesk 3ds Max [S]

187
Seer [T]
Adobe Photoshop, Autodesk 3ds Max [S]

Amir Zand

188
Taking Care of Gods [T]
Adobe Photoshop [S] KADOKAWA [C]
Tamako Gunji [E] Liu Cixin [A]

189
Perhaps the Stars [T]
Adobe Photoshop, Cinema 4D [S] Tor Books [C]
Ada Palmer [A]

Darwin Cellis

190–191
Arid Block [T]
3DCoat, Adobe Photoshop, Blender [S]

Josef Surý (LEVELIST4)

ARTIFICIAL PORTAL

Josef Surý (LEVELIST4)

ARTIFICIAL PORTAL

194–195
Post-apocalyptic City [T]
Adobe Photoshop, Blender [S]

Stanislav Verbitsky

196-197
Rogue Chariot [T]
Blender [S]

Stanislav Verbitsky

ARTIFICIAL PORTAL

198–199
Rogue Chariot [T]
Blender [S]

Stanislav Verbitsky

Elia Pellegrini

XuTeng Pan

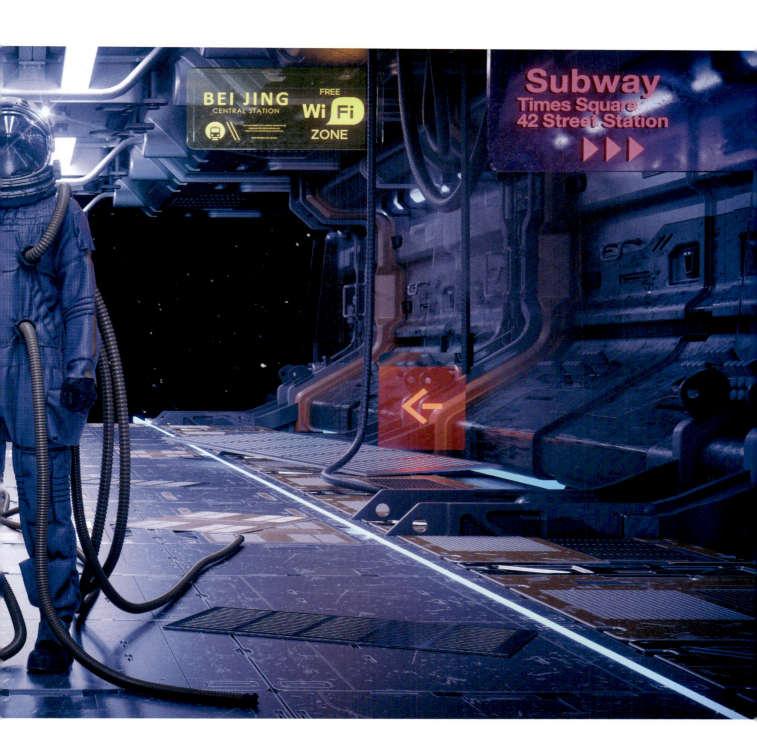

BEI JING
CENTRAL STATION

FREE
Wi Fi
ZONE

Subway
Times Square
42 Street Station
▶ ▶ ▶

Stanislav Verbitsky

Stanislav Verbitsky

210-211
The Catcher — Pods [T]
Adobe Photoshop (matte painting),
Chaos V-Ray, SketchUp [S]

Tom Burkewitz

212
The Catcher — Depot [T]
Adobe Photoshop (matte painting),
Chaos V-Ray, SketchUp [S]

213
The Catcher — Temple [T]
Adobe Photoshop (matte painting),
Chaos V-Ray, SketchUp [S]

Tom Burkewitz

Daniele Gay

214–215
New Day [T]
Adobe Photoshop, Daz Studio [S]

Thu Berchs

216–217
Kirkwood Towers [T]
3DCoat, Adobe Photoshop [S]
Wojtek Fus [SC]

Mahdi Abderrahim

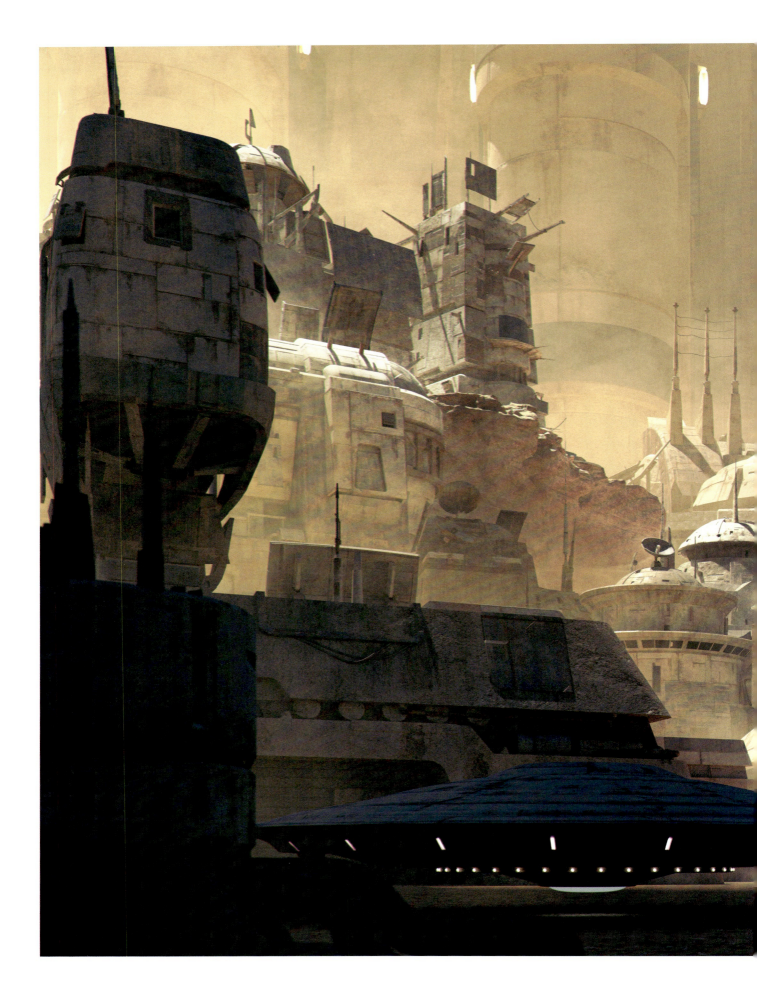

Daniele Gay

Qin Shi

Leo Li

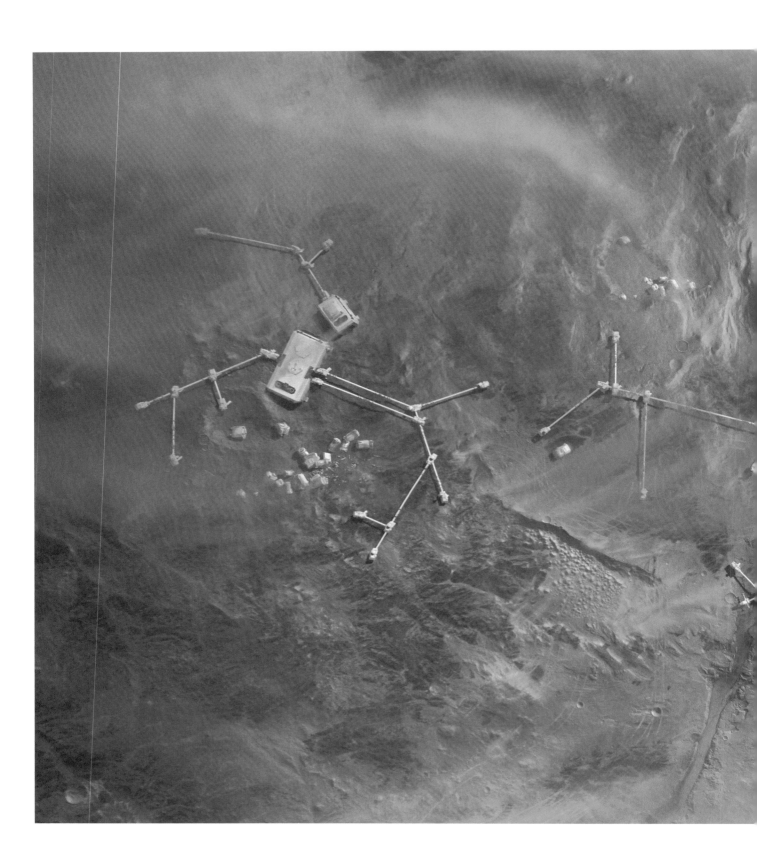

Andrii Vasyliev

Leo Li

228–229
The Wreckage [T]
Adobe Photoshop, Blender [S]

Thomas Puggelli

230–231
Rendez-vous [T]
Adobe Photoshop, Blender [S]
Obhéa Editions [C]

Thomas Puggelli

232–233
Untitled [T]
Adobe Photoshop, Blender [S]
Obhéa Editions [C]

Amir Zand

Giulia Gentilini

236–237
Nice Machine at Work [T]
Adobe Photoshop, Blender [S]

Donchenko Volodymyr

238–239
"Matrix 4: Reboot" Fan Art — 3D Award [T]
Adobe Photoshop, Autodesk 3ds Max, Chaos Corona [S]

Ede László

240–241
Old Exhaust Port [T]
3DCoat, Adobe Photoshop, Blender, Cinema 4D, OctaneRender [S]

Pablo Muñoz Gómez

Icy Exoplanet Concept [T]
Adobe Photoshop, Blender, Procreate, ZBrush [S]

Pablo Muñoz Gómez

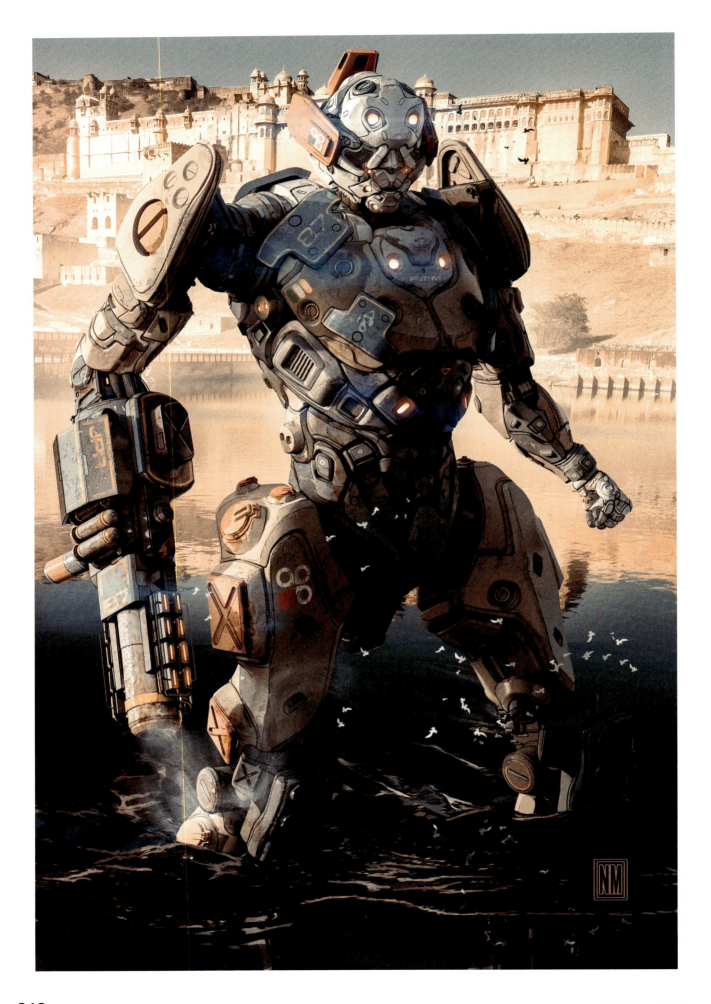

Neeraj Menon

246
Prthvi [T]
Adobe Photoshop, KeyShot, ZBrush [S]

247
Alley Rat [T]
Adobe Photoshop, KeyShot, ZBrush [S]

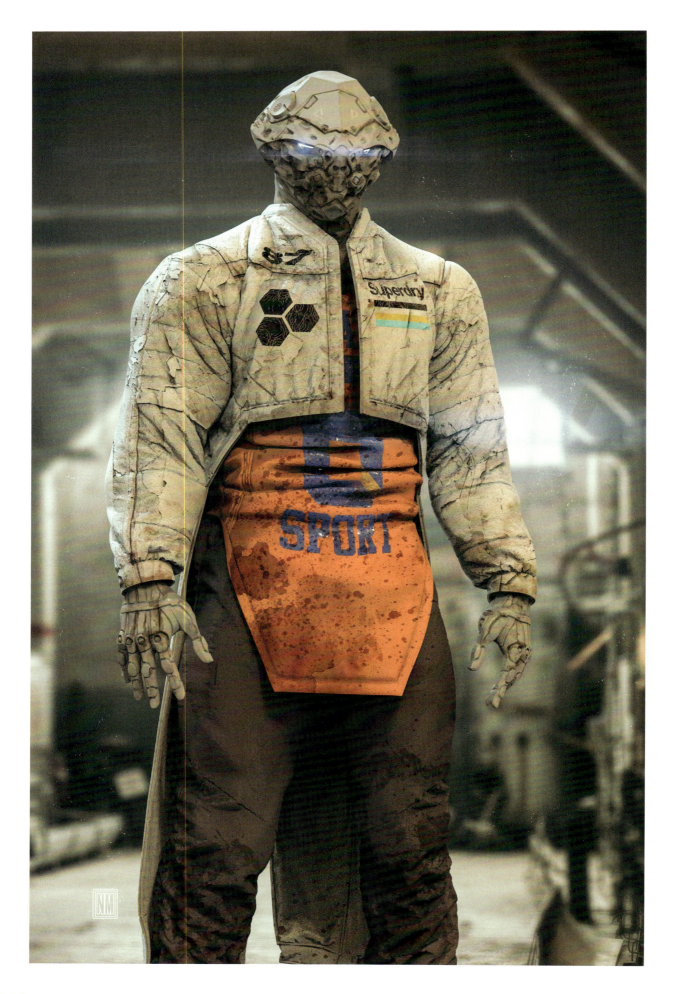

Neeraj Menon

248
Warehouse [T]
Adobe Photoshop, KeyShot,
Marvelous Designer, ZBrush [S]

249
Hallway Staredown [T]
Adobe Photoshop, KeyShot,
Marvelous Designer, ZBrush [S]

250
Untitled [T]
Adobe Photoshop [S]

Thomas Puggelli

BIOGRAPHY

Albert Ramon Puig

Albert Ramon Puig has been working in the video game industry for 12 years, having started in mobile games and moving onto PC and console games. With a love for Sci-Fi, he is currently in the midst of a personal project to create a retro-futuristic universe by designing planets, civilisations, technology, and more.

Amir Zand

Amir Zand is a multidisciplinary digital artist specialising in concept design and illustration. His work has been featured in books, magazines, and exhibitions. He has also designed over 50 book covers and contributed illustrations to renowned universes such as Star Wars, Warhammer 40k, DUNE, Halo, Mortal Engines, and Wandering Earth.

Andrii Vasyliev

Andrii Vasyliev is a Ukrainian digital artist who specialises in matte painting, concept art, and illustration for movies and games.

Dangiuz

Known by his pseudonym Dangiuz, Leopoldo D'Angelo is a Turin-based contemporary visual artist, digital artist, and art director who specialises in Sci-Fi themes.

Daniele Gay

With an affinity for fantasy and horror, Daniele has been working in digital art since 2008. Her path has also drawn her to the mysterious charm of UFOs and aliens, as well as 3D work. Her montages have appeared on multiple book covers and high-tech magazines.

Darwin Cellis

With a passion for creating bizarre worlds and unique visual designs, Darwin began drawing since childhood. He eventually moved into a career as a graphic designer, which he has been honing professionally for over 20 years. As a constant learner, he recently ventured into the creation of concept art while inspired by the art, music, and pop culture of the '80s and '90s.

Darya Laziuk

Darya is a freelance environment concept artist based in Warsaw. Inspired by nature, movies, games, and great artists, she uses 3D modelling, kitbashing, photobashing, and digital drawing in her work.

Dmytro Bessonov

Dmytro Bessonov, a Ukrainian concept artist with over a decade of industry experience, has contributed to diverse projects, including film pitches and video games. Despite a challenging path without formal technical training, he acquired expertise through work, courses, and mentorships. Committed to aiding beginners, he now offers free feedback to make their journey smoother.

Domenico Sellaro

Domenico Sellaro is a concept artist, digital matte painter, and environment artist for films and video games. He has been working on several projects for different companies such as DreamWorks, Wizard of the Coast, Dazzle Pictures, Room8 Studio, UPP, Jellyfish Pictures, Passion Pictures, We Are Royale, Stormind Games, and the like.

Donchenko Volodymyr

Donchenko Volodymyr is a senior environment concept artist with a focus on concept formation and schematic design through selecting reference images, building 3ds Max models and doing photoreel image renderings with post work in Photoshop. In his spare time, he enjoys swimming, running, travelling, and photography.

Ede László

Ede László is a Hungarian freelance digital artist who works in the movie and game industry. He is currently working at Terraform as a senior environment concept artist.

Elia Pellegrini

Elia Pellegrini is an Italian artist represented by Noruwei as well as a musician. She specialises in drawing, painting, and digital art, and currently works as a freelance CGI and VFX artist. Deeply inspired by the epic and ancient concepts derived from her dreams, her work is typically surrealistic in nature and revolves around time, light, and love.

Fang Yi

Fang Yi is a design enthusiast with years of experience in the film and visual effects industry. In recent years, Their stylistic emphasis has been predominantly centered on crafting realistic Sci-Fi designs and universes.

Filip Hodas

Filip Hodas is a 3D artist based in Prague. In his work, Filip balances on the edge between reality and fiction with elaborate, detailed renderings. He is most known for his series "Pop Culture Dystopia", which envisions decaying pop-culture icons in desolate and abandoned post-apocalyptic landscapes.

BIOGRAPHY

Gal Barkan

Gal Barkan is a visual designer, art director, and musician. He creates artwork featuring detailed futuristic neon metropolises and fantasy worlds, inspired by Sci-Fi films, space and cosmology, music, visual arts, and nature.

Giulia Gentilini

Giulia Gentilini is a concept artist and illustrator with experience in video games, short movies, and tabletop role-playing games. Passionate about her work, Giulia is always looking for new ways to improve her skills.

Hardy Fowler

Hardy Fowler is a concept artist and illustrator with over a decade of industry experience working for dozens of clients. His credits include Neon District (Blockade Games), Games Workshop, and Disney. He is also the founder of the online art school Digital Painting Studio.

Hélio Frazão

Helio Frazao is a concept artist, illustrator, and art director based in Leiria. Inspired by cyberpunk-inspired environments, he currently works at Volta on a number of undisclosed projects.

Jarvinart

Known as Jarvinart, Idil Dursun, a Turkish architect and CG artist, specialises in crafting expansive Sci-Fi and dystopian landscapes. In building her unique universe, she envisions a future world through striking concept artworks. Her creations have garnered recognition in esteemed platforms such as Dark Matter Magazine, W1 Curates, Pellas Gallery in the US, and Dart Museum – Permanente di Milano.

Josef Surý (LEVELIST4)

Josef Surý is a concept designer and visual artist who is known in the world of digital art under the pseudonym LEVELIST4. His style is characterised by dynamic compositions, Sci-Fi environments, and futuristic architecture. Over time, this has led him to create fantastical worlds for clients around the world. He currently works as a freelance environment concept artist.

Lazaro

Lazaro is the alias of Umberto Votta, a digital artist based in Milan who creates work in 3D and post-produced in Photoshop. He also enjoys creating Sci-Fi worlds infused with cyberpunk and dystopian elements.

Leo Li

Leo Li is a concept artist working in the video game industry with a specialisation in illustration and concept design. He also works as a concept artist at Tesla, supporting designs for cars, robots, and architecture as well as visualising pre-production concept designs. He loves creating personal projects that explore Sci-Fi, fantasy, and multicultural worlds.

Mahdi Abderrahim

Mahdi is a matte painter and visualiser influenced by the likes of landscapes, astronomy, and Sci-Fi.

Neeraj Menon

Neeraj Menon is an award-winning freelance concept artist, illustrator, and comic book colourist based in Pune. With a degree in communication design majoring in animation from the Symbiosis Institute of Design, he worked as a colourist for comic publishers worldwide. He has also worked as a concept artist for creatures, robots, vehicles, and more.

Pablo Muñoz Gómez

Pablo Muñoz Gómez is a 3D concept and character artist with a passion for education. His work involves 3D sculpting, visual development, and other mixed-media projects. He is the founder of the ZBrushGuides website, the 3Dconceptartist academy and the 3DSnippets project — platforms that showcase his work and workflows that help other artists level up their skills.

Petter Steen

Petter Steen is a Swede self-taught VFX artist who has been based in London for the past 15 years. He is currently working as a senior generalist at Industrial Light & Magic.

Qin Shi

Formerly a 3D designer at NetEase, Qin Shi currently works as a freelance game level and 3D artist, specialising in modelling, texturing, compositing, and crafting special effects. Qin has an affinity for Western popular culture, including mecha, horror, post-apocalyptic universes, and the many genres of Sci-Fi.

Sergii Golotovskyi

Sergii Golotovskyi is a concept designer with more than 5 years of experience in the film and game industry. He also has a master's degree in architecture and urban planning, and he specialises in environmental and architectural concept design. He has worked for studios such as Netflix, Netease, NCsoft, ArenaNet, Blinkink, FinalStrikeGames, and more.

Space Meerkat

Space Meerkat is the pseudonym of Rene Ipša, a specialist in 3D modelling, rendering and animation. Rene has worked with Blender to create various 3D models and renders of interiors, furniture, and various products and characters.

Stanislav Verbitsky

Stanislav Verbitsky is a 3D concept artist working in the game industry. He specialises in Sci-Fi environment and space art, but also has an affinity with fantasy.

Thomas Puggelli

Thomas Puggelli has been a Sci-Fi enthusiast since childhood, and he specialises in crafting cinematic landscapes. His art explores the captivating contrast of scale between characters and scenic elements, be they natural or artificial. He focuses on creating landmarks and artificial marvels, inviting viewers to join him and his characters in immersive journeys through imaginative realms.

Thu Berchs

Thu Berchs is a senior concept artist currently working at NetEase Games. Having grown up surrounded by his astronomer parents and space-related books, he started his career as an artist at the age of 22 with a passion for outer space.

Tom Burkewitz

Born in 1981, Tom Burkewitz is a Riga-based architect and digital artist with more than 12 years of experience in digital imagery and architecture.

Tom Hisbergue

Tom Hisbergue is a French concept artist who currently works at Asobo studio. He was previously a digital matte painter with 10 years of experience in the VFX industry for live and animated movies.

Vladimir Manyukhin

Vladimir Manyukhin is based in Moscow and has worked in the art industry for more than 20 years. He has been affiliated with video game developer Creative Assembly and created artwork for games and films such as "Total War: Warhammer". He has also drawn various covers in the fantasy and Sci-Fi genre that have been published worldwide.

Xiangzhao Xi

After graduating from the animation department of Tianjin Academy of Fine Arts, Xiangzhao Xi joined the game industry and was employed by NetEase and Tencent.

XuTeng Pan

XuTeng Pan is a post-90s visual designer from Xi'an, engaged in visual work in videos, games, and music. Early in his career, he focused on the game and illustration industry, then transformed from an independent game developer to a visual designer and art director with a focus on design. He is currently producing independent creative work.